Travel Journal

Name _____

Volume _____

Beginning Date _____

End Date _____

Ideas for Journaling

Cover Page and Spine of Book: Record name, volume and beginning date of this volume. Record end date when book is full. Other covers are available if you want another volume. Search for *S M Travel Journals*.

Travels: Record the date and destination, of each trip, or if you are visiting multiple cities in one trip, each city can have its own chapter, whichever way you would like. Up to 32 different trips/destinations can be entered.

Maps: You can color in, or label the continents, oceans, countries, territories or states that you visit. I suggest colored pencils. The maps are not perfect, but hopefully you will still find them useful.

Destination: A trip name, (ex: Bahamas Cruise), or actual place/town you visit.

Date: Record beginning date to end date of trip or day/time in the destination.

Who: People you travel with, or new people you meet.

Places: Any other cities, suburbs or areas you visit, like downtown or waterfront.

Accommodations: Where you stay/sleep.

Transportation: Any type of transportation, subway, train, plane, boat, rental car, or maybe you tried something new.

Food/Restaurants: Any interesting food or restaurant you wish to remember.

Sightseeing: Any landmark or historical sight, museums, ball parks, parks or specific place you visit.

Souvenirs: Any souvenirs you want to remember, for you or someone else.

Other Costs: Subway tickets, museum tickets, price of anything you wish to remember.

Best Part of Trip: Whatever you think was the best part of the trip.

Daily Notes or Pictures: You can write out day by day, or draw pictures, (again, I suggest colored pencils), or both. However you wish to record your memories.

For added protection when traveling, journal will fit in a large zip lock bag.
Happy Travels

Travels

Where I've been (maps)   6

Date	Destination	Page
_____	_____	136
_____	_____	142
_____	_____	148
_____	_____	154
_____	_____	160
_____	_____	166
_____	_____	172
_____	_____	178
_____	_____	184
_____	_____	190
_____	_____	196
_____	_____	202

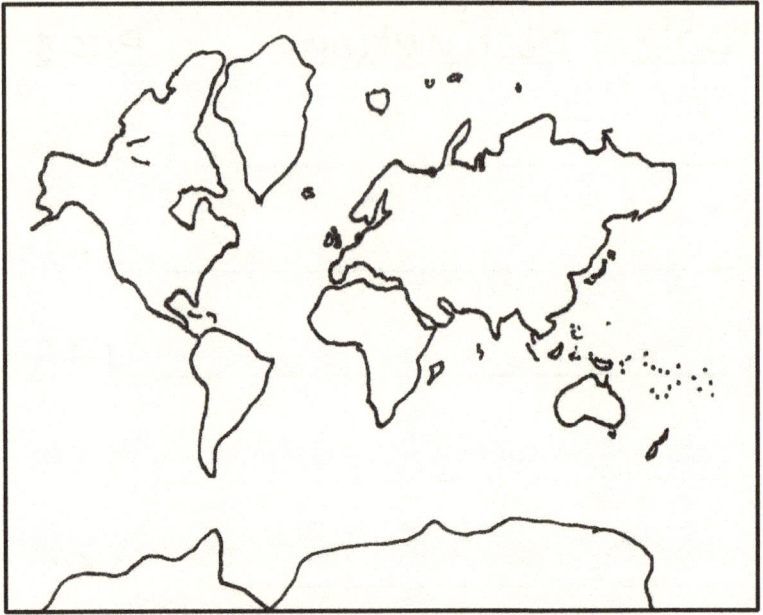

World Map

Continents	Oceans
Africa	Atlantic Ocean
Antarctica	Arctic Ocean
Asia	Indian Ocean
Australia	Pacific Ocean
Europe	Southern Ocean
North America	
South America	

Africa

Asia

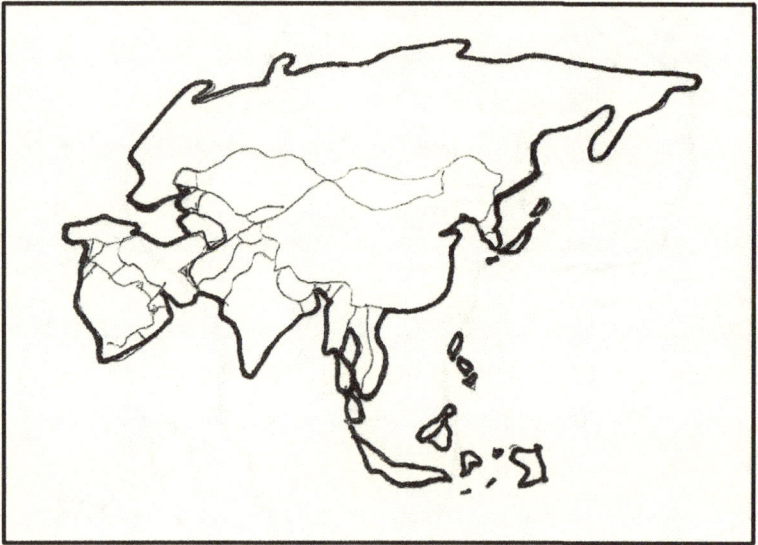

Australia and

Oceania

Europe

North America

South America

United States

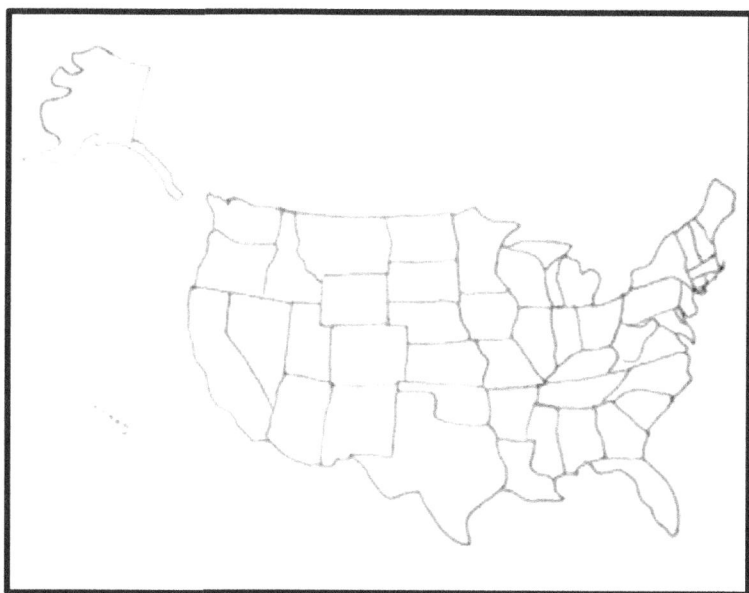

Other Map Notes

Travels

Destination _____

_____

Date _____

Who _____

_____

Places _____

_____

_____

Accommodations _____

_____

_____

Transportation _____

_____

_____

Food and Restaurants _____

_____

_____

_____

Sightseeing _____

_____

_____

_____

_____

_____

Souvenirs _____

_____

_____

Other Costs _____

_____

_____

Best Part of the Trip _____

_____

_____

_____

_____

_____

Daily Notes or Pictures

Daily Notes or Pictures

Daily Notes or Pictures

Daily Notes or Pictures

Destination _____

_____

Date _____

Who _____

_____

Places _____

_____

_____

Accommodations _____

_____

_____

Transportation _____

_____

_____

Food and Restaurants _____

_____

_____

_____

Sightseeing _____

_____

_____

_____

_____

Souvenirs _____

_____

_____

Other Costs _____

_____

_____

Best Part of the Trip _____

_____

_____

_____

_____

_____

Daily Notes or Pictures

Daily Notes or Pictures

Daily Notes or Pictures

Daily Notes or Pictures

Destination _____

_____

Date _____

Who _____

_____

Places _____

_____

_____

Accommodations _____

_____

_____

Transportation _____

_____

_____

Food and Restaurants _____

_____

_____

_____

Sightseeing _____

_____

_____

_____

_____

_____

Souvenirs _____

_____

_____

Other Costs _____

_____

_____

Best Part of the Trip _____

_____

_____

_____

_____

_____

Daily Notes or Pictures

Daily Notes or Pictures

Daily Notes or Pictures

Daily Notes or Pictures

Destination _____

_____

Date _____

Who _____

_____

Places _____

_____

_____

Accommodations _____

_____

_____

Transportation _____

_____

_____

Food and Restaurants _____

_____

_____

_____

Sightseeing _____

_____

_____

_____

_____

Souvenirs _____

_____

_____

Other Costs _____

_____

_____

Best Part of the Trip _____

_____

_____

_____

_____

_____

Daily Notes or Pictures

Daily Notes or Pictures

Daily Notes or Pictures

Daily Notes or Pictures

Destination _____

_____

Date _____
Who _____

_____

Places _____

_____

_____

Accommodations _____

_____

_____

Transportation _____

_____

_____

Food and Restaurants _____

_____

_____

_____

Sightseeing _____

_____

_____

_____

_____

_____

Souvenirs _____

_____

_____

Other Costs _____

_____

_____

Best Part of the Trip _____

_____

_____

_____

_____

_____

Daily Notes or Pictures

Daily Notes or Pictures

Daily Notes or Pictures

Daily Notes or Pictures

Destination _____

_____

Date _____
Who _____

_____

Places _____

_____

_____

Accommodations _____

_____

_____

Transportation _____

_____

_____

Food and Restaurants _____

_____

_____

_____

Sightseeing _____

_____

_____

_____

_____

_____

Souvenirs _____

_____

_____

Other Costs _____

_____

_____

Best Part of the Trip _____

_____

_____

_____

_____

_____

Daily Notes or Pictures

Daily Notes or Pictures

Daily Notes or Pictures

Daily Notes or Pictures

Destination _____

_____

Date _____

Who _____

_____

Places _____

_____

_____

Accommodations _____

_____

_____

Transportation _____

_____

_____

Food and Restaurants _____

_____

_____

_____

Sightseeing _____

_____

_____

_____

_____

_____

Souvenirs _____

_____

_____

Other Costs _____

_____

_____

Best Part of the Trip _____

_____

_____

_____

_____

_____

Daily Notes or Pictures

Daily Notes or Pictures

Daily Notes or Pictures

Daily Notes or Pictures

Destination _____

_____

Date _____

Who _____

_____

Places _____

_____

_____

Accommodations _____

_____

_____

Transportation _____

_____

_____

Food and Restaurants _____

_____

_____

_____

Sightseeing _____

_____

_____

_____

_____

Souvenirs _____

_____

_____

Other Costs _____

_____

_____

Best Part of the Trip _____

_____

_____

_____

_____

_____

Daily Notes or Pictures

Daily Notes or Pictures

Daily Notes or Pictures

Daily Notes or Pictures

Destination _____

_____

Date _____

Who _____

_____

Places _____

_____

_____

Accommodations _____

_____

_____

Transportation _____

_____

_____

Food and Restaurants _____

_____

_____

_____

Sightseeing _____

_____

_____

_____

_____

_____

Souvenirs _____

_____

_____

Other Costs _____

_____

_____

Best Part of the Trip _____

_____

_____

_____

_____

_____

Daily Notes or Pictures

Daily Notes or Pictures

Daily Notes or Pictures

Daily Notes or Pictures

Destination _____

_____

Date _____

Who _____

_____

Places _____

_____

_____

Accommodations _____

_____

_____

Transportation _____

_____

_____

Food and Restaurants _____

_____

_____

_____

Sightseeing _____

_____

_____

_____

_____

_____

Souvenirs _____

_____

_____

Other Costs _____

_____

_____

Best Part of the Trip _____

_____

_____

_____

_____

_____

Daily Notes or Pictures

Daily Notes or Pictures

Daily Notes or Pictures

Daily Notes or Pictures

Destination _____

_____

Date _____
Who _____

_____

Places _____

_____

_____

Accommodations _____

_____

_____

Transportation _____

_____

_____

Food and Restaurants _____

_____

_____

_____

Sightseeing _____

_____

_____

_____

_____

_____

Souvenirs _____

_____

_____

Other Costs _____

_____

_____

Best Part of the Trip _____

_____

_____

_____

_____

_____

Daily Notes or Pictures

Daily Notes or Pictures

Daily Notes or Pictures

Daily Notes or Pictures

Destination _____

_____

Date _____
Who _____

_____

Places _____

_____

_____

Accommodations _____

_____

_____

Transportation _____

_____

_____

Food and Restaurants _____

_____

_____

_____

Sightseeing _____

_____

_____

_____

_____

_____

Souvenirs _____

_____

_____

Other Costs _____

_____

_____

Best Part of the Trip _____

_____

_____

_____

_____

_____

Daily Notes or Pictures

Daily Notes or Pictures

Daily Notes or Pictures

Daily Notes or Pictures

Destination _____

_____

Date _____
Who _____

_____

Places _____

_____

_____

Accommodations _____

_____

_____

Transportation _____

_____

_____

Food and Restaurants _____

_____

_____

_____

Sightseeing _____

_____

_____

_____

_____

_____

Souvenirs _____

_____

_____

Other Costs _____

_____

_____

Best Part of the Trip _____

_____

_____

_____

_____

_____

Daily Notes or Pictures

Daily Notes or Pictures

Daily Notes or Pictures

Daily Notes or Pictures

Destination _____

_____

Date _____

Who _____

_____

Places _____

_____

_____

Accommodations _____

_____

_____

Transportation _____

_____

_____

Food and Restaurants _____

_____

_____

_____

Sightseeing _____

_____

_____

_____

_____

_____

Souvenirs _____

_____

_____

Other Costs _____

_____

_____

Best Part of the Trip _____

_____

_____

_____

_____

_____

Daily Notes or Pictures

Daily Notes or Pictures

Daily Notes or Pictures

Daily Notes or Pictures

Destination _____

_____

Date _____
Who _____

_____

Places _____

_____

_____

Accommodations _____

_____

_____

Transportation _____

_____

_____

Food and Restaurants _____

_____

_____

_____

Sightseeing _____

_____

_____

_____

_____

_____

Souvenirs _____

_____

_____

Other Costs _____

_____

_____

Best Part of the Trip _____

_____

_____

_____

_____

_____

Daily Notes or Pictures

Daily Notes or Pictures

Daily Notes or Pictures

Daily Notes or Pictures

Destination _____

_____

Date _____

Who _____

_____

Places _____

_____

_____

Accommodations _____

_____

_____

Transportation _____

_____

_____

Food and Restaurants _____

_____

_____

_____

Sightseeing _____

_____

_____

_____

_____

_____

Souvenirs _____

_____

_____

Other Costs _____

_____

_____

Best Part of the Trip _____

_____

_____

_____

_____

_____

Daily Notes or Pictures

Daily Notes or Pictures

Daily Notes or Pictures

Daily Notes or Pictures

Destination _____

_____

Date _____

Who _____

_____

Places _____

_____

_____

Accommodations _____

_____

_____

Transportation _____

_____

_____

Food and Restaurants _____

_____

_____

_____

Sightseeing _____

_____

_____

_____

_____

Souvenirs _____

_____

_____

Other Costs _____

_____

_____

Best Part of the Trip _____

_____

_____

_____

_____

_____

Daily Notes or Pictures

Daily Notes or Pictures

Daily Notes or Pictures

Daily Notes or Pictures

Destination _____

_____

Date _____
Who _____

_____

Places _____

_____

_____

Accommodations _____

_____

_____

Transportation _____

_____

_____

Food and Restaurants _____

_____

_____

_____

Sightseeing _____

_____

_____

_____

_____

_____

Souvenirs _____

_____

_____

Other Costs _____

_____

_____

Best Part of the Trip _____

_____

_____

_____

_____

_____

Daily Notes or Pictures

Daily Notes or Pictures

Daily Notes or Pictures

Daily Notes or Pictures

Destination _____

_____

Date _____

Who _____

_____

Places _____

_____

_____

Accommodations _____

_____

_____

Transportation _____

_____

_____

Food and Restaurants _____

_____

_____

_____

Sightseeing _____

_____

_____

_____

_____

_____

Souvenirs _____

_____

_____

Other Costs _____

_____

_____

Best Part of the Trip _____

_____

_____

_____

_____

_____

Daily Notes or Pictures

Daily Notes or Pictures

Daily Notes or Pictures

Daily Notes or Pictures

Destination _____

_____

Date _____
Who _____

_____

Places _____

_____

_____

Accommodations _____

_____

_____

Transportation _____

_____

_____

Food and Restaurants _____

_____

_____

_____

Sightseeing _____

_____

_____

_____

_____

_____

Souvenirs _____

_____

_____

Other Costs _____

_____

_____

Best Part of the Trip _____

_____

_____

_____

_____

_____

Daily Notes or Pictures

Daily Notes or Pictures

Daily Notes or Pictures

Daily Notes or Pictures

Destination _____

_____

Date _____
Who _____

_____

Places _____

_____

_____

Accommodations _____

_____

_____

Transportation _____

_____

_____

Food and Restaurants _____

_____

_____

_____

Sightseeing _____

_____

_____

_____

_____

_____

Souvenirs _____

_____

_____

Other Costs _____

_____

_____

Best Part of the Trip _____

_____

_____

_____

_____

_____

Daily Notes or Pictures

Daily Notes or Pictures

Daily Notes or Pictures

Daily Notes or Pictures

Destination _____

_____

Date _____

Who _____

_____

Places _____

_____

_____

Accommodations _____

_____

_____

Transportation _____

_____

_____

Food and Restaurants _____

_____

_____

_____

Sightseeing _____

_____

_____

_____

_____

Souvenirs _____

_____

_____

Other Costs _____

_____

_____

Best Part of the Trip _____

_____

_____

_____

_____

_____

Daily Notes or Pictures

Daily Notes or Pictures

Daily Notes or Pictures

Daily Notes or Pictures

Destination _____

_____

Date _____

Who _____

_____

Places _____

_____

_____

Accommodations _____

_____

_____

Transportation _____

_____

_____

Food and Restaurants _____

_____

_____

_____

Sightseeing _____

_____

_____

_____

_____

_____

Souvenirs _____

_____

_____

Other Costs _____

_____

_____

Best Part of the Trip _____

_____

_____

_____

_____

_____

Daily Notes or Pictures

Daily Notes or Pictures

Daily Notes or Pictures

Daily Notes or Pictures

Destination _____

_____

Date _____

Who _____

_____

Places _____

_____

_____

Accommodations _____

_____

_____

Transportation _____

_____

_____

Food and Restaurants _____

_____

_____

_____

Sightseeing _____

_____

_____

_____

_____

_____

Souvenirs _____

_____

_____

Other Costs _____

_____

_____

Best Part of the Trip _____

_____

_____

_____

_____

_____

Daily Notes or Pictures

Daily Notes or Pictures

Daily Notes or Pictures

Daily Notes or Pictures

Destination _____

_____

Date _____

Who _____

_____

Places _____

_____

_____

Accommodations _____

_____

_____

Transportation _____

_____

_____

Food and Restaurants _____

_____

_____

_____

Sightseeing _____

_____

_____

_____

_____

_____

Souvenirs _____

_____

_____

Other Costs _____

_____

_____

Best Part of the Trip _____

_____

_____

_____

_____

_____

Daily Notes or Pictures

Daily Notes or Pictures

Daily Notes or Pictures

Daily Notes or Pictures

Destination _____

_____

Date _____

Who _____

_____

Places _____

_____

_____

Accommodations _____

_____

_____

Transportation _____

_____

_____

Food and Restaurants _____

_____

_____

_____

Sightseeing _____

_____

_____

_____

_____

_____

Souvenirs _____

_____

_____

Other Costs _____

_____

_____

Best Part of the Trip _____

_____

_____

_____

_____

_____

Daily Notes or Pictures

Daily Notes or Pictures

Daily Notes or Pictures

Daily Notes or Pictures

Destination _____

_____

Date _____

Who _____

_____

Places _____

_____

_____

Accommodations _____

_____

_____

Transportation _____

_____

_____

Food and Restaurants _____

_____

_____

_____

Sightseeing _____

_____

_____

_____

_____

_____

Souvenirs _____

_____

_____

Other Costs _____

_____

_____

Best Part of the Trip _____

_____

_____

_____

_____

_____

Daily Notes or Pictures

Daily Notes or Pictures

Daily Notes or Pictures

Daily Notes or Pictures

Destination _____

_____

Date _____

Who _____

_____

Places _____

_____

_____

Accommodations _____

_____

_____

Transportation _____

_____

_____

Food and Restaurants _____

_____

_____

_____

Sightseeing _____

_____

_____

_____

_____

_____

Souvenirs _____

_____

_____

Other Costs _____

_____

_____

Best Part of the Trip _____

_____

_____

_____

_____

_____

Daily Notes or Pictures

Daily Notes or Pictures

Daily Notes or Pictures

Daily Notes or Pictures

Destination _____

_____

Date _____
Who _____

_____

Places _____

_____

_____

Accommodations _____

_____

_____

Transportation _____

_____

_____

Food and Restaurants _____

_____

_____

_____

Sightseeing _____

_____

_____

_____

_____

_____

Souvenirs _____

_____

_____

Other Costs _____

_____

_____

Best Part of the Trip _____

_____

_____

_____

_____

Daily Notes or Pictures

Daily Notes or Pictures

Daily Notes or Pictures

Daily Notes or Pictures

Destination _____

_____

Date _____

Who _____

_____

Places _____

_____

_____

Accommodations _____

_____

_____

Transportation _____

_____

_____

Food and Restaurants _____

_____

_____

_____

Sightseeing _____

_____

_____

_____

_____

_____

Souvenirs _____

_____

_____

Other Costs _____

_____

_____

Best Part of the Trip _____

_____

_____

_____

_____

_____

Daily Notes or Pictures

Daily Notes or Pictures

Daily Notes or Pictures

Daily Notes or Pictures

Destination _____

_____

Date _____
Who _____

_____

Places _____

_____

_____

Accommodations _____

_____

_____

Transportation _____

_____

_____

Food and Restaurants _____

_____

_____

_____

Sightseeing _____

_____

_____

_____

_____

_____

Souvenirs _____

_____

_____

Other Costs _____

_____

_____

Best Part of the Trip _____

_____

_____

_____

_____

_____

Daily Notes or Pictures

Daily Notes or Pictures

Daily Notes or Pictures

Daily Notes or Pictures

Destination _____

_____

Date _____
Who _____

_____

Places _____

_____

_____

Accommodations _____

_____

_____

Transportation _____

_____

_____

Food and Restaurants _____

_____

_____

_____

Sightseeing _____

_____

_____

_____

_____

Souvenirs _____

_____

Other Costs _____

_____

Best Part of the Trip _____

_____

_____

_____

_____

Daily Notes or Pictures

Daily Notes or Pictures

Daily Notes or Pictures

Daily Notes or Pictures

Made in the USA
Las Vegas, NV
23 September 2023

78022604R00121